Grammar
Ad Libs

P9-AGT-071

Table of Contents

Grammar Ad Libs

Designed to supplement your classroom literacy program, *Grammar Ad Libs* is also ideal for learning centers or for at-home practice. With assistance, children of varying ability levels can enjoy these activities and begin to understand two basic principles: each word has a different function in a sentence (parts of speech), and sentences are built in certain predictable ways (sentence construction).

You may wish to review the parts of speech with your children before beginning the activities, and brainstorm examples of the types of words they may be asked to think of. Activities in the first half of this book ask for different types of nouns, verbs, adjectives, and adverbs. Prepositions are introduced in the second part of the book when the focus changes from building words to building sentences and identifying parts of speech.

Note: A well-timed mini-lesson on challenging issues, such as using -s or -es to pluralize a word (*fox* to *foxes*), or choosing between the articles *a* and *an*, may be very effective when children hear something that sounds wrong or see something that looks wrong after inserting their words into the stories. Children may also insert the inappropriate tense or form of a verb into their stories (past vs. present, singular vs. plural). Encourage them to listen for subject-verb agreement as you (or they) read their stories aloud, and demonstrate how to correct grammar as these opportunities arise.

Teaching Notes: Word Parts

This section includes page sets for each word-construction skill (for example, synonyms). The Warm-Up pages in this section provide children with word choices and extra guidance for completing the activity. The page that follows each Warm-Up page encourages children to apply their understanding of word-building and spelling concepts.

As you introduce each activity, call children's attention to the skills that are featured on the page, and provide examples of them. "We will be practicing synonyms, or words that have the same meaning, on this page. One pair of synonyms is *angry* and *mad.* Can you think of another pair of synonyms, or words that have the same meaning?" Ask children to brainstorm other synonyms. Then read the directions on the activity page. It may be helpful to read instructions aloud to early readers and help them think of words to use in the story. Higher-level readers may be able to select their own words without assistance, and they may wish to use a dictionary or thesaurus as a source for word ideas.

The prefix and suffix activities may be more difficult for some children. On these pages, we've included a Word Bank or a word list at the bottom of the page. You may choose to obscure this section before photocopying.

> Pages 4 through 23 target the following skills:
>
> - Identifying words that have the same meaning (synonyms)
> - Identifying words that have opposite meanings (antonyms)
> - Recognizing and forming compound words by combining smaller words
> - Identifying and building words with prefixes (*uni-, bi-, tri-, tele-, out-, re-, pre-, un-, im-, in-*) and base words
> - Identifying and building words with suffixes (*-ly, -est, -er, -ing, -ness, -less, -ful, -en, -er*) and base words
> - Recognizing misspelled words and correcting the spelling errors

All children should transfer their word choices into the blanks in the story. Then you can read the stories aloud, or invite volunteers to share their stories with the class. Use each silly story as a lesson by pointing out word families and spelling patterns, and discussing children's word choices.

© Learning Resources, Inc.

Synonyms Ad Libs Warm-Up

Synonyms are words that mean the same thing. Choose a synonym for each underlined word, and circle it.

1. afraid: scared worried terrified

2. big: large huge gigantic

3. cold: chilly freezing icy

4. broken: damaged smashed ruined

5. friend: pal buddy chum

6. nice: kind caring thoughtful

7. wet: drippy drenched soaked

8. good: wonderful great nice

Eddy and Max

Max was very _____. During the storm, a
                (1)

_____ gust of _____ wind had _____ a
   (2)   (3)   (4)

window in his garage, and he was home by himself!

He wasn't sure what to do. Luckily, Max's _____
                                              (5)

Eddy lived right next door. Eddy was a very _____
                                               (6)

guy, so he helped Max clean up the _____ broken
                                       (7)

glass from the window and cover it with cardboard.

Isn't it _____ to have a friend like Eddy?
            (8)

© Learning Resources, Inc.   Grammar Ad Libs

Name:_____

Synonyms Ad Libs

Think of a synonym for each word, and write it on the line.

1. home _____

2. fast _____

3. crabby _____

4. walked _____

5. shout _____

6. good _____

7. grin _____

Late for my Lesson

I had to get to my _____, and _____! I was
(1)   (2)

late for my piano lesson with my _____ old teacher,
(3)

Mr. Snit. If I _____ through the door just a minute
(4)

late, Mr. Snit would _____ and wave his hands,
(5)

and complain that I would never be a _____ piano
(6)

player. I pedaled my bike _____ly and saw my
(2)

house up ahead. But Mr. Snit wasn't waiting for me at

the window. He was walking up the driveway! He was

late, too! "I had car trouble," he growled with a frown. I

could not hide my _____.
(7)

Name:_____

Antonyms Ad Libs Warm-Up

Antonyms are words that have opposite meanings. Choose an antonym for each underlined word and circle it.

1. light: bright   dingy   dark

2. down: around   up   through

3. ran: walked   sprinted   jumped

4. short: small   huge   tall

5. closed: shut   entered   opened

6. noisily: loudly   quietly   happily

7. rough: smooth   bumpy   sharp

8. deep: shallow   thick   empty

9. dry: thin   wet   crusty

Sneaking a Swim

One night at summer camp, we decided it was time for

an adventure. When the camp was _____, we
(1)

sneaked out of our cabin and headed _____ into
(2)

the woods. We _____ through the _____ grass
(3)   (4)

for a few minutes until we reached a fence. We

_____ the gate and _____ closed it again. Then
(5)   (6)

we walked over the _____ stones on the edge of the
(7)

beach. We splashed in the _____ water for a
(8)

while, then walked back to camp, _____ but happy.
(9)

© Learning Resources, Inc.   Grammar Ad Libs

Antonyms Ad Libs

Think of an antonym for each word, and write it on the line.

1. sour _____

2. easy _____

3. Over _____

4. worst _____

5. Clean _____

6. up _____

7. left _____

8. less _____

9. lose _____

10. sat _____

The _____ Taste of Victory
(1)

We had a _____ soccer game last night! _____
(2)   (3)

the stars, we played the _____ team in the league,
(4)

the _____ Dragons! We were _____ by a point
(5)   (6)

when Mike kicked the ball with his _____ foot and
(7)

scored a goal. We just needed one _____ point to
(8)

_____ the game! The rest of us _____ and
(9)   (10)

watched as our team scored again! We celebrated our

_____ victory with ice cream.
(1)

Grammar Ad Libs   © Learning Resources, Inc.

Compound Words Ad Libs 1 Warm-Up

Choose one compound word from each category, and circle it.

1. animal compound word: catfish   bluebird   groundhog

2. thing compound word: skateboard   baseball   flowerpot

3. place compound word: doghouse   bathtub   ballpark

4. food compound word: cupcake   grapefruit   doughnut

5. vehicle compound word: spaceship   sailboat   motorcycle

The Earthquake

I was in my bedroom with my _____, Toots, when we
$\qquad$ (1)

felt the house shake. It was an earthquake! I grabbed Toots

and my favorite _____, and hurried towards the
$\qquad$ (2)

_____, where I knew we'd be safe. I grabbed a
(3)

_____ from the kitchen in case we got hungry. Toots
(4)

and I stayed in the _____ until a man in a
(3)

_____ told us it was over.
(5)

Compound Words Ad Libs 1

Build compound words that make sense by combining two words in each row and writing the new words on the lines in the story.

1. thing compound word: ache   tooth   head   pain
2. place compound word: room   bath   bed   tub
3. thing compound word: ball   man   snow   mobile
4. body part compound word: eye   ball   lid   lash
5. thing compound word: color   melon   water   fall
6. food compound word: berry   straw   blue   fish

Curing a _____
(1)

To get rid of a painful _____, follow these easy
                              (1)

steps. First of all, find a quiet _____ in which you
                                    (2)

can lie down comfortably. Try not to think about your

_____ or your homework, and you will begin to
  (3)

relax. Rub your _____ gently, and focus on a
                   (4)

_____. You may even wish to snack on a dish of
  (5)

homemade _____ jam and cornbread. Soon you
              (6)

will feel your _____ disappear.
                 (1)

Compound Words Ad Libs 2 Warm-Up

Choose one compound word from each category, and circle it.

1. thing compound word:	highchair	broomstick	teapot
2. thing compound word:	schoolyard	campfire	flagpole
3. describing compound word:	upright	overtired	worthwhile
4. place compound word:	birdhouse	fishbowl	rowboat
5. foods compound word:	peanuts	pancakes	gingerbread
6. person compound word:	cowboy	policewoman	firefighter
7. clothing compound word:	sweatshirt	underwear	necklace

My Sunday Afternoon

On Sundays I like to polish my _____ collection quietly
(1)

while I daydream about dancing around the _____. But
(2)

last Sunday, everything went wrong. First, my most _____
(3)

_____ got stuck in the _____, and I had to pry it
(1)   (4)

out with a clothespin. Then, my grandmother dropped

_____ on the same _____, and it took me two hours
(5)   (1)

to clean it. And if that wasn't enough, a _____ burst into
(6)

my bedroom just as I was changing my _____! I hope
(7)

next Sunday is better!

© Learning Resources, Inc. Grammar Ad Libs

Name:_____

Compound Words Ad Libs 2

Build compound words that make sense by combining two words in each row and writing the new words on the lines in the story.

1. thing compound word:	flower	sun	set	room
2. place compound word:	room	bath	bed	tub
3. thing compound word:	shelf	worm	book	note
4. thing compound word:	light	band	head	line
5. things compound word:	tea	cups	spoons	pots

Annabelle's Dollhouse

Annabelle's dollhouse is the best one I've ever seen. It

has a _____, lots of tables and chairs, and the
         (1)

_____ is big enough for two people to sit in it!
    (2)

Each wall has its own _____ — in fact, Annabelle
                              (3)

keeps her _____ collection on the _____ by the
              (4)   (3)

doormat! The dollhouse kitchen is filled with everything

you would find in a regular kitchen, even _____!
                                              (5)

© Learning Resources, Inc.

Name:_____

Prefixes *uni-, bi-, tri-, tele-, out-* Ad Libs Warm-Up

Read the definition of each word. Look at the words in the word bank. Choose the word that best fits the definition, and write it on the line.

1. dinosaur with three horns:_____

2. outfit with two pieces:_____

3. thing with two wheels:_____

4. thing with one wheel:_____

5. thing to use to speak to someone from a distance:_____

6. thing with a screen that we watch from a distance:_____

7. action word that means to get to be too big for something:_____

Word Bank

bicycle   triceratops   television

unicycle   telephone   outgrow

bikini

The _____ in the Outfield
(1)

The player in right field is a _____! She wears a
(1)

_____ instead of a uniform because she thinks it's
(2)

more comfortable. Why does she ride a _____? It's
(3)

because her _____ has a flat tire! Our baseball
(4)

coach gets a lot of _____ calls from _____
(5)   (6)

reporters who want to interview our team. They know

that someday our triceratops will _____ her
(7)

baseball mitt, and her days in right field will be over!

© Learning Resources, Inc.   Grammar Ad Libs

Name:_____

Prefixes uni-, bi-, tri-, tele-, out- Ad Libs

Read the definition of each word. Look at the words in the word bank. Choose the word that best fits the definition, and write it on the line.

1. action word that means running faster than someone:_____

2. thing you look through to see things from a distance:_____

3. matching outfits that a group of people wear:_____

4. creatures with one horn:_____

5. thing with three legs:_____

6. group of three:_____

7. shape with three sides:_____

Word Bank

triangle   uniforms   trio

telescope   tripod

unicorns   outrunning

_____ the _____
     (1)   (4)

_____ are very fast creatures. One evening, I set my
  (4)

_____ up on its three-legged _____ so I could
  (2)   (5)

look at the beautiful stars. Suddenly, a _____ of
                                              (6)

_____ came running into the _____ near me,
  (4)   (7)

wearing Yankees _____. They challenged me to a
                      (3)

race. We took our places, then set off running. I realized

soon that I was _____ these speedy unicorns! I won
                     (1)

the race easily. I must be pretty speedy, too!

Grammar Ad Libs

© Learning Resources, Inc.

13

Name:_____

Read the definition of each word. Look at the words in the word bank.
Choose the word that best fits the definition, and write it on the line.

1. action word that means to heat before:_____

2. action word that means to mix before:_____

3. describing word that means not correct:_____

4. describing word that means not perfect:_____

5. action word that means to mix again:_____

6. describing word that means not cooked:_____

7. describing word that means not safe:_____

Word Bank

remix

unsafe

premix

preheat

uncooked

incorrect

imperfect

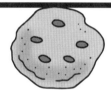

Baking Cookies

First, _____ the oven. Then _____ the dry
     (1)   (2)

ingredients. Do not mix everything at once — that would

be _____ and _____! Next, beat the butter and
   (3)   (4)

eggs together. _____ the dry ingredients and add
         (5)

them to the butter and eggs. Do not eat the _____
             (6)

cookie dough, because it is _____. Put balls of dough
       (7)

on a cookie sheet and bake them in the oven. Enjoy!

 © Learning Resources, Inc. Grammar Ad Libs

Prefixes re-, pre-, un-, im-, in- Ad Libs

Read the definition of each word. Look at the words in the word bank. Choose the word that best fits the definition, and write it on the line.

1. -ly word that means not happily:_____

2. describing word that means not polite:_____

3. action word that means to sort before:_____

4. action word that means to soak before:_____

5. action word that means to wash again:_____

6. describing word that means not visible:_____

Word Bank

rewash

presoak

presort

unhappily

invisible

impolite

Andy's Pink Laundry

Andy walked _____, wearing pink socks and pants.
(1)

I didn't mean to be _____, but I asked, "Why are
(2)

you wearing pink clothes?" He said, "I always

_____ and _____ my clothes, but my sister's
(3)   (4)

red shirt got mixed in with my clothes and turned them

all pink! I tried to _____ the clothes, but it didn't
(5)

help. I wish I was _____," sighed Andy.
(6)

15

 © Learning Resources, Inc.

Name: _____

Suffixes -ly, -est Ad Libs Warm-Up

Add the -ly suffix to each word, and read the new words aloud.

1. odd _____

2. sad _____

3. strong _____

4. quick _____

Add the -est suffix to each word, and read the new words aloud.

5. ripe _____

6. fresh _____

 The _____ Vegetables
(6)

_____ enough, it is difficult to buy fresh vegetables
(1)

today. Many vegetables in the grocery store have been

_____ sitting in their bins for weeks! I would
(2)

_____ recommend that you find a local vegetable
(3)

stand or small store and _____ purchase your
(4)

veggies there. You will find the _____ tomatoes
(5)

and onions. The farmers will be glad to

tell you all about their _____ vegetables.
(6)

© Learning Resources, Inc. Grammar Ad Libs

Suffixes -ly, -est Ad Libs

Think of four words that end with *-ly*, and write them on lines 1-4. Then think of four words that end with *-est* and write them on lines 5-8.

-ly words

1. _____
2. _____
3. _____
4. _____

-est words

5. _____
6. _____
7. _____
8. _____

At the Races

Good afternoon! I'd _____ like to welcome you to the

(1)

racetrack, and I hope that you will enjoy our _____

(5)

race of the afternoon! The horses are ready for the start of

the race, and they're off! _____, Zoe's Pony has taken

(2)

the lead. Fast Frieda and Chocolate Thunder are following

_____ behind. And the _____ horse in the race is

(3)   (6)

Prince Longnose, who is _____ bringing up the rear.

(4)

Who will be the _____? It's Chocolate Thunder! She is

(7)

the _____ horse in the country!

(8)

© Learning Resources, Inc.

Name:_____

Noun Suffixes -er, -ing, -ness Ad Libs Warm-Up

Add the -er suffix to each word, and read the new words aloud.

1. teach_____   2. sing_____   3. wait_____

Add the –ness suffix to each word, and read the new words aloud.

4. good_____   5. sad_____

Add the –ing suffix to each word, and read the new words aloud.

6.stuff_____   7. frost_____

The Right Job for You

What is the right job for you? _____s help children
                                    (1)

learn reading, writing, and lessons about _____.
                                                (4)

_____s travel all over, mostly to sing about love
   (2)

and _____. _____s spend much of their day
       (5)   (3)

bringing the perfect turkey _____ and cake
                                 (6)

_____ to their customers. All would be interesting
   (7)

jobs.

© Learning Resources, Inc.

Grammar Ad Libs

Noun Suffixes -er, -ing, -ness Ad Libs

Think of two words that end with *-er* (like *teacher*), and write them on lines 1 and 2. Then think of two words that end with *-ing* (like *frosting*) and write them on lines 3 and 4. Finally, think of two words that end with *-ness* (like *goodness*), and write them on lines 5 and 6.

-er words	*-ing* words	*-ness* words
1. _____	3. _____	5. _____
2. _____	4. _____	6. _____

Strangeness on the Bus

I met an interesting _____ on the bus. He was an
$\qquad$ (1)

odd fellow who talked about his _____ the whole
$\qquad$ (3)

time! Out of the _____ of my heart, I listened to the
$\qquad$ (5)

_____ go on and on about his precious _____.
(1) $\qquad$ (3)

I told him I was a _____ from down the street. He
$\qquad$ (2)

ignored me and talked about _____. I shook my
$\qquad$ (4)

head in _____ and got off the bus.
$\qquad$ (6)

-ness words: craziness, gladness, happiness, kindness, madness, silliness

-ing words: bedding, painting, roofing

-er words: baker, drummer, farmer, painter, reporter, swimmer

© Learning Resources, Inc.

Name:_____

Add the *-less* suffix to each word, and read the new words aloud:

1. hope_____   2. tooth_____   3. bottom_____

Add the *-ful* suffix to each word: 4. wonder_____   5. force_____

Add the *-er* suffix to this word: 6. smart_____

Add the *-en* suffix to each word: 7. gold _____   8. wool _____

Colt Dashing and the _____ Troll
(2)

I saw a _____ movie last weekend called Colt
(4)

Dashing and the _____ Troll. Colt Dashing is on a
(2)

_____ journey through the deep and _____
(1)   (5)

waters of the Nile, searching for the famous _____
(7)

egg of Cairo. His enemy, a _____ troll called Tito,
(2)

wants it, too. Colt is _____ than the troll and finds
(6)

the egg in a _____ pit of snakes. He smuggles the
(3)

egg out of Egypt in a _____ carpet and brings it to
(8)

Texas, where it belongs.

© Learning Resources, Inc.
Grammar Ad Libs

Name:_____

Adjective Suffixes -less, -ful, -en, -er Ad Libs

Think of two words that end with -less (like *hopeless*), and write them on lines 1 and 2. Then think of two words that end with -ful (like *wonderful*), and write them on lines 3 and 4. Think of two words that end with -en (like *golden*), and write them on lines 5 and 6. Finally, think of two words that end with -er (like *smarter*), and write them on lines 7 and 8.

-less words	-ful words	-en words	-er words
1. _____	3. _____	5. _____	7. _____
2. _____	4. _____	6. _____	8. _____

Catching a _____ Snake
(1)

If you see a _____ snake, be _____. Take a
(1)   (3)

_____ shovel or rake, and try to scoop up the
(5)

_____ snake in a _____ way. If that
(2)   (4)

doesn't work, you may need to use a _____ item,
(7)

such as a _____ spoon or chopsticks. Remember
(5)

that the snake is _____ than you, so move slowly
(8)

and cautiously around it.

-er words: brighter, cleaner, dumber, faster, father, stronger, uglier

-en words: broken, hidden, frozen, wooden

-ful words: graceful, grateful, helpful, hopeful, joyful, thoughtful, thankful

-less words: boneless, brainless, careless, clueless, headless, worthless

Grammar Ad Libs   © Learning Resources, Inc.

Name:_____

Misspelled Words Ad Libs

Find the word in each category that is spelled correctly, and circle it.

1. thing: chicken   chickin   chikin

2. describing word: favrit   favorite   favorit

3. thing: anamal   animal   animel

4. adverb: alwayz   alwaze   always

5. things: frends   freinds   friends

6. adverb: finally   finaly   finly

7. action word: agrey   agree   aggree

My _____ _____
       (2)   (3)

The _____ is my _____ _____ because it
      (1)   (2)   (3)

_____ makes me laugh. My _____ and I enjoy
   (4)   (5)

chasing and playing with the _____s, and _____
                                (1)   (6)

feeding them at night. Today I forgot to feed them until ten

o'clock! Most people would _____ that ten o'clock
                              (7)

isn't that late, but the chickens were very angry. When I let

them out, they all pecked at my knees! Ow!

© Learning Resources, Inc.   Grammar Ad Libs

Name: _____

More Misspelled Words Ad Libs

Find the word in each category that is spelled correctly, and circle it.

1. thing: monkee   munkey   monkey

2. describing word: young   yung   younge

3. action word: cryd   cried   cryed

4. thing: balloon   baloon   ballon

5. action word: thought   thaught   thawt

6. action word: bot   bought   bawt

7. adverb: truly   truely   truley

8. action word: surprised   suprised   saprized

The Naughty _____
(1)

Matt's little brother, Ben, is very _____. At the zoo,
(2)

Ben _____ because he wanted a red _____.
(3)   (4)

Matt _____ about it, then _____ a _____
(5)   (6)   (4)

for Ben. When the _____ spotted Ben's red
(1)

_____, it grabbed it and ran away. Matt was
(4)

_____ worried that Ben would cry again, but Ben
(7)

_____ him and laughed.
(8)

     © Learning Resources, Inc.

Teaching Notes: Sentence Parts

This section devotes two pages to each of five parts of speech (nouns, verbs, adjectives, adverbs, and prepositions). As you introduce each activity, call children's attention to the part of speech that is featured on the page, and provide examples of it. "The part of speech we will be learning about today is a noun. Nouns are words that are people, places, or things. Some examples of nouns include *iguana*, *library*, *doctors*, and *sister*. Can you think of any other examples of nouns?" Explain that children will be asked to think of different nouns and write them in the stories.

Read the directions on each activity page, and encourage children to select words at the top of the page without looking at the story below. It may be helpful to read the word choices on the Warm-Up pages aloud to early readers, and allow them to listen and choose. Higher-level readers may be able to read and select words without assistance. All children should transfer their word choices into the blanks in the story. Then you can read the stories aloud, or invite volunteers to share their stories with the class.

Pages 26 through 48 target the following skills:

- Identifying nouns as words that name people, places, and things

- Identifying verbs as action words

- Identifying adjectives as words that describe nouns (or pronouns)

- Identifying adverbs as words that describe verbs, adjectives, or other adverbs

- Identifying prepositions as words that relate nouns (or pronouns) to another word

- Incorporating nouns, verbs, adjectives, adverbs, and prepositions into sentences

- Understanding basic sentence structure

As appropriate, present mini-lessons on topics such as spelling changes, tense, and agreement as children complete the activity pages or share their stories. For example, you may wish to discuss *y*-to-*i* changes (*baby* to *babies*) as children pluralize nouns on the noun pages. A mini-lesson on subject-verb agreement or tense may be helpful as children select and insert verbs into their stories on the verb pages. And a short lesson about matching articles to nouns (*a* lion/*an* elephant) would be appropriate as children work on many of the pages. Need-based grammatical instruction or review can be highly effective when it is properly timed.

If children have difficulty thinking of their own words to use on some pages, refer them to the word choices on the Warm-Up pages, supply them with a list of words from which they can choose, or allow them to work with partners to generate words. Word Walls that feature groups of nouns, verbs, adverbs, etc. may also serve as a helpful reference for these activities. Encourage children to add words to the Word Wall as they see them in print or hear them used in sentences. Use the following lists of words to help inspire children as they complete the activity pages or to start a Word Wall in your classroom.

© Learning Resources, Inc.

Parts of Speech Word Lists

Nouns

People: baby, babysitter, barber, biker, brother, burglar, clown, cousin, dentist, driver, firefighter, friend, goalie, husband, lady, maid, mailman, manager, mother, neighbor, pilot, rabbi, saleswoman, teacher, teenager, uncle, veterinarian, writer, zookeeper

Places: airport, aquarium, bakery, bank, bathroom, birdcage, city, church, class, cottage, country, doghouse, garden, highway, hospital, hotel, house, island, kitchen, library, mall, mountain, office, pantry, park, party, pool, school, store, tent, theater, train, wedding, zoo

Things: basketball, bicycle, caboose, candle, cannon, cereal, chocolate, dictionary, earring, furnace, game, garbage, gasoline, hippopotamus, lace, laughter, money, monster, nose, parrot, pickle, pizza, rain, sandwich, shovel, sofa, soup, stamp, tinfoil, tulip, turtle, tuba

Verbs

begin, buy, chat, cheat, chew, cook, count, cut, dance, deny, distract, drag, drop, dump, dunk, fry, gobble, hike, invent, jog, keep, leap, open, paddle, play, praise, punch, quit, scream, sniff, speed, spin, spit, sprint, stitch, swim, swing, teach, think, toss, waddle, wander, work, zip

Adjectives

busy, cheap, disappointed, dumb, early, eleven, five, fluffy, fragile, freezing, gentle, grateful, hard, important, itchy, lucky, mature, narrow, old, plaid, plump, purple, round, red, rich, rubbery, silly, slow, speedy, speckled, stretchy, striped, thick, wet, wrong, young

Adverbs

almost, always, confidently, crabbily, dangerously, definitely, doubtfully, ever, fondly, gladly, grossly, gruffly, happily, hotly, loudly, madly, quietly, oddly, really, reluctantly, slowly, sometimes, soon, still, sweetly, tomorrow, triumphantly, yesterday

Prepositions

above, about, across, after, against, along, around, at, away, before, between, beyond, by, down, during, even, for, from, in, into, near, next, of, off, on, out, over, since, through, to, toward, under, until, up, upon, with, without

© Learning Resources, Inc.

Name:_____

Nouns Ad Libs Warm-Up

Nouns are words that name people, places, or things. Choose one noun from each group, and circle it.

1. noun (person):   janitor   referee   firefighter

2. noun (place):   bridge   pool   zoo

3. noun (thing):   zebra   turkey   cheetah

4. noun (person):   girl   grandmother   babysitter

5. noun (thing):   purse   umbrella   glove

6. noun (thing):   flag   hose   mop

7. plural noun (persons): skaters   clowns   dentists

An Unlikely Superhero

The fearless Super_____ enjoys helping others and
                 (1)

fighting crime. I saw him leaping over the new city

_____ faster than a flying _____. He swooped
  (2)   (3)

down to assist a small _____ who had lost her
                     (4)

_____, and then flew away. Minutes later,
  (5)

Super_____ waved his magical _____ to help
       (1)   (6)

some _____. They cheered with joy!
    (7)

© Learning Resources, Inc.   Grammar Ad Libs

Nouns Ad Libs

Think of some nouns, and write them on the lines.

1. noun (place):_____

2. noun (thing):_____

3. plural noun (things):_____

4. noun (person):_____

5. plural noun (things):_____

6. plural noun (things):_____

7. noun (place):_____

A Day at the _____
(1)

Yesterday, I visited the local _____ to enjoy the
(1)

_____ and scenery. For lunch, I stopped in a café
(2)

and ate delicious _____ and milk. I talked to a
(3)

friendly _____ who sold _____. She and I
(4) (5)

soon realized that we both collect _____, so we
(6)

agreed to meet at the _____ when she was done
(7)

working. I am excited about my new friend.

Name:_____

Verbs Ad Libs Warm-Up

Directions: Verbs are action words. Choose one verb from each group, and circle it.

1. verb: glide   gallop   bound   5. verb: kiss   tickle   pet

2. verb: lead   teach   ask   6. verb: looking laughing   pointing

3. verb: doing   following performing   7. verb: sew   relax   sleep

4. verb: brush   wash   cuddle

Learning to_____
(1)

You can _____ your horse to _____ beautifully
(2)   (1)

by _____ these easy steps. First, _____ your
(3)   (4)

horse gently. Tell him he is beautiful, and _____
(5)

him behind the ears. Then lead your horse around in a

circle, demonstrating how to _____. Your horse will
(1)

learn how to _____ by _____ at you. Then sit
(1)   (6)

back and _____, and your horse will _____
(7)   (1)

around happily.

© Learning Resources, Inc.   Grammar Ad Libs

Verbs Ad Libs

Directions: Think of some verbs, and write them on the lines. Use the verbs in the word bank if you need some help.

1. verb: _____

2. verb: _____

3. verb: _____

4. verb: _____

5. verb: _____

6. verb: _____

7. verb: _____

8. verb: _____

Word Bank

jump	boogie
write	spray
chew	steal
wash	sweep
wiggle	crumble
feed	wipe

The Chore List

My mother _____ed me quite a chore list! I'll never
_____(1)_____

finish them all!

- Empty the wastebaskets and _____ them.
  _____(2)_____

- _____ the flowers.
  _____(3)_____

- _____ your brother while he naps.
  _____(4)_____

- _____ the dirty dishes in the sink.
  _____(5)_____

- Walk to the store and _____ a new broom.
  _____(6)_____

- _____ the dog and _____ the cat.
  _____(7)_____   _____(8)_____

© Learning Resources, Inc.

Grammar Ad Libs 1 Warm-Up

Choose one noun or verb from each group, and circle it.

1. noun (place):	store	factory	parade
2. plural noun (things):	fish	banjos	notebooks
3. verb:	paddle	wander	glide
4. verb:	swat	tap	kick
5. verb:	grunt	spit	laugh
6. plural noun (things):	trumpets	mushrooms	acorns

Sarah's Summer Job

Sarah works at the _____ where they make _____!
(1)   (2)

It's great because she can _____ around the building all
(3)

day, checking on the machines that _____ and package
(4)

the _____. She gets three breaks a day and as many
(2)

free _____ as she can carry home. Sarah knows the
(2)

secret to making great _____ is to _____ at them
(2)   (5)

with _____ as they are packaged. Now Sarah likes to
(6)

_____ at everything she sees!
(5)

© Learning Resources, Inc.

Name:_____

Grammar Ad Libs 1

Directions: Think of some nouns and verbs, and write them on the lines.

1. plural noun (things):_____

2. noun (place):_____

3. verb:_____

4. plural noun (things):_____

5. verb:_____

6. noun (thing):_____

7. noun (person):_____

Stranded on a _____
(2)

Our ship ran out of _____, so we're stuck on this
(1)

hot tropical _____, with no water to _____
(2)   (3)

or _____ to eat. The hot sun tires us and
(4)

_____ our skin. We sleep on the ship's _____
(5)   (6)

every night, which isn't comfortable. The ship's

_____ tells us that we will be rescued any day
(7)

now, but I don't trust him. After all, he's the one who

got us into this mess!

Grammar Ad Libs 2 Warm-Up

Choose one noun or verb from each group, and circle it.

1. noun (place): circus   jungle   mansion

2. noun (thing): kazoo   teepee   snorkel

3. verb: pulled   tossed   took

4. verb: chirped   fell   jumped

5. plural noun (things): ferns   xylophones   giraffes

6. plural noun (things): helmets   hamburgers   lanterns

7. plural noun (things): snails   plums   yo-yos

The Haunted _____
(1)

My friends and I had to check out the haunted

_____. James brought his _____ just in case,
(1)   (2)

and we _____ our bikes to the edge of town. The
(3)

spooky old _____ was behind a thick group of
(1)

_____, which James bravely led us through. He
(5)

_____ slowly, and we followed behind him,
(4)

waving our _____ so we could see. We weren't
(6)

scared until we heard a sound: "WWEEEEEOOOO!"

We ran from that _____ faster than _____!
(1)   (7)

© Learning Resources, Inc.

Grammar Ad-Libs 2

Think of some nouns and verbs, and write them on the lines.

1. verb: _____

2. verb: _____

3. plural noun (things): _____

4. plural noun (persons): _____

5. verb: _____

6. noun (thing): _____

7. plural noun (things): _____

Staying in Shape

To stay in shape and _____ your body,
(1)

you should _____ several times a week and eat
(2)

healthy _____. _____ recommend that you
(3)   (4)

_____ a few miles each day and stretch properly
(5)

when you finish. Then do some basic _____-lifting.
(6)

Lift two 5-pound _____s until you are exhausted.
(6)

Follow up your exercise routine with a healthy meal of

fruit juice, _____, and vegetables. You will feel
(7)

great!

© Learning Resources, Inc.

Adjectives Ad Libs Warm-Up

Adjectives are words that describe nouns. Choose one adjective from each group, and circle it.

1. adjective: yellow brown green
2. adjective: huge empty cold
3. adjective: silly odd funny

4. adjective: cheap crumpled itchy
5. adjective: sharp dazzling clumsy
6. adjective: wild hairy weird

Who Is That Guy?

A _____-haired man poked his head out of a
(1)

manhole on the street today as I walked home from my

_____ school. That seemed very _____ to me.
(2)   (3)

I followed him. He walked quickly, stopping only to

take off a _____ coat and toss it into the bushes
(4)

near my neighbor's house. Then he made a _____
(5)

turn and disappeared down a narrow alley. I began to

realize something _____, though . . . that man
(6)

was my principal!

© Learning Resources, Inc.

Name: _____

Adjectives Ad Libs

Think of some adjectives, and write them on the lines.

1. adjective: _____   4. adjective: _____   7. adjective: _____

2. adjective: _____   5. adjective: _____   8. adjective: _____

3. adjective: _____   6. adjective: _____

Transforming Your _____ Dog
(1)

If your dog is _____, you can try several things to
(1)

make him more _____. First, make sure your dog
(2)

isn't _____ when you begin working with him.
(3)

Feed him, give him plenty of _____ water, and
(4)

make sure he had a _____ night's sleep. Try to
(5)

encourage your dog to be more _____ around
(6)

you and other people. Introduce him to a _____
(7)

leash, and use it around the house. Soon your dog will

be a _____ pet!
(8)

© Learning Resources, Inc.

Adverbs Ad Libs Warm-Up

Adverbs are words that usually describe verbs. Choose one adverb from each group, and circle it.

1. adverb: quickly messily loudly
2. adverb: gently firmly strangely
3. adverb: always usually often

4. adverb: dangerously clumsily horribly
5. adverb: happily sadly kindly
6. adverb: secretly sneakily rudely

Madeline in the Tree

"Madeline, come down _____," said Julia
(1)

_____. She was tired of babysitting for Madeline,
(2)

who _____ got into trouble. Madeline was
(3)

perched in an oak tree in the front yard, with her legs

dangling _____ over the street. "Please come
(4)

down or you could get hurt. I've made some cookies

for you," said Julia _____. Madeline climbed
(5)

down, and went inside to find her cookies. Julia

laughed _____. She had tricked Madeline!
(6)

Name: _____

Adverbs Ad Libs

Think of some adverbs, and write them on the lines. Use the adverbs in the word bank if you need some help.

1. adverb: _____   4. adverb: _____

2. adverb: _____   5. adverb: _____

3. adverb: _____   6. adverb: _____

Word Bank

slowly	suddenly
energetically	dumbly
nicely	wickedly
neatly	lovingly
calmly	quietly

 Runaway Car

I was relaxing _____ on my porch, when
(1)

_____ a car began to roll _____ towards my
(2) (3)

house! I _____ jumped up and ran towards the
(4)

car. There was no driver inside! Luckily, I am very fast,

and I _____ placed my hand through the open
(5)

window and turned the steering wheel. The runaway

car almost hit my house, but my plan worked out

_____. A disaster was prevented. Whew!
(6)

Name:_____

Prepositions Ad Libs 1

Prepositions are words that link nouns to other words. Choose one preposition from each group, and circle it.

1. preposition: out   through   outside

2. preposition: into   by   in

3. preposition: under   over   across

4. preposition: near   to   around

5. preposition: into   for   toward

Zippy and the Bathrobe

I looked _____ my window and saw my father
(1)

running _____ our backyard with his towel
(2)

_____ his waist! I watched him run _____ the
(3)   (4)

sandbox, stop, change directions, and head _____
(5)

the swimming pool. Then I realized that our dog Zippy

had my father's bathrobe in his mouth! Dad was

chasing Zippy to get his robe back!

© Learning Resources, Inc.

Prepositions Ad Libs 2

Prepositions are words that link nouns to other words. Choose one preposition from each group, and circle it.

1. preposition: to   for   in
2. preposition: into   in   for
3. preposition: on   along   between
4. preposition: beside   onto   to
5. preposition: on   below   in

Building a Birdhouse

Birdhouses are simple to build and are a nice addition

_____ any yard. You will need wood, a saw, a
　　(1)

hammer, nails, and some glue. Use the saw to cut the

wood _____ six-inch pieces. Place glue
　　　　(2)

_____ the pieces of wood, and hold them in place
　　(3)

until the glue dries. Then, use the hammer and nails to

fasten the pieces of wood _____ each other more
　　　　　　　　　　　(4)

permanently. When your birdhouse is dry, you can

hang it _____ a tree.
　　　(5)

© Learning Resources, Inc.

Grammar Ad Libs 3 Warm-Up

Choose one word from each group, and circle it.

1. noun (thing): watch harmonica spoon

2. noun (place): gymnasium park zoo

3. adjective: large pink striped

4. preposition: under into beside

5. verb: jiggled crunched tossed

6. adverb: carefully silently restlessly

7. verb: cry snore wiggle

8. noun (thing): lunchbox armpit yogurt

The Lost _____
(1)

I got halfway home from the _____ before I realized
(2)

that my _____ _____ was missing. I had placed
(3)   (1)

it _____ my pocket before I left, but I must have
(4)

_____ it on my way home. I _____ retraced my
(5)   (6)

steps to the _____, but I didn't find my _____.
(2)   (1)

I was sure my parents would _____ when I told
(7)

them it was missing. In desperation, I jammed my hands

into my _____, and guess what I found!
(8)

Grammar Ad Libs 3

Think of a word for each category, and write it on the line.

1. noun (animal): _____

2. adjective: _____

3. adverb: _____

4. verb: _____

5. adjective: _____

6. verb: _____

7. preposition: _____

8. verb: _____

Choosing a _____
(1)

Selecting a pet _____ should be a _____ and
(1)   (2)

careful process. _____ choose a place from which
(3)

you'd like to purchase your _____. Ask to see all
(1)

of the _____s they have, and _____ each
(1)   (4)

_____ with _____ hands and a calm voice.
(1)   (5)

Never _____ a _____ _____ a corner, or
(6)   (1)   (7)

the _____ may _____! Most importantly,
(1)   (8)

choose a _____ that seems loyal and friendly.
(1)

  © Learning Resources, Inc.

Name:_____

Grammar Ad Libs 4 Warm-Up

Directions: Choose one word from each group, and circle it.

1. adjective: bright   windy   snowy

2. verb: dancing   shouting   peeking

3. adjective: slippery   green   stinky

4. adjective: weird   nervous   hyper

5. adverb: quickly   sadly   angrily

6. verb: teased   counted   poked

7. preposition: in   on   beside

8. verb: boogying   scraping   twirling

Winning the Race

Our team trained for the relay race for months, but we never dreamed that we could win! The day of the race was _____ (1) and clear. The sun was _____ (2) from behind the clouds, and as we stepped to the _____ (3) running track, I felt very _____ (4). I _____ (5) _____ (6) my teammates to make sure everyone was _____ (7) the right spot. Then, the race began! I remember the sound of my feet _____ (8) on the track, and the incredible joy I felt when my team crossed the finish line first. It was a great day!

© Learning Resources, Inc.

Grammar Ad Libs 4

Think of a word for each category, and write it on the line.

1. adjective: _____

2. noun (place): _____

3. adverb: _____

4. verb: _____

5. plural noun (things): _____

6. preposition: _____

7. plural noun (things): _____

8. adverb: _____

9. verb: _____

A Desert Hike

Mark and his _____ dad took a 50-mile hike
(1)

through the hot deserts of the _____ last summer.
(2)

For days, they _____ _____ down steep slopes,
(3)   (4)

through dusty _____ and _____ rough paths.
(5)   (6)

At times, Mark said his feet felt like _____, but he
(7)

_____ learned to ignore the discomfort and
(8)

_____ the plants and animals around him.
(9)

© Learning Resources, Inc.

Grammar Ad Libs 5 Warm-Up

Choose one word from each group, and circle it.

1. adjective: spicy curly interesting

2. verb: flying leaping reading

3. adverb: silently wetly frantically

4. verb: coughed hollered burped

5. noun (thing): box slipper tube

6. preposition: under beneath by

7. noun (thing): cheese oil glue

8. plural noun (things): candies plates forks

The Restaurant Disaster

It is a _____ idea to bring a raccoon into a restaurant.
(1)

I saw a young raccoon _____ _____ by the road
(2)   (3)

one night and _____ until my parents stopped the car.
(4)

Then I ran to the raccoon and put him into an empty

_____ to keep him safe. No one noticed that I brought
(5)

him into the restaurant with us and set him _____ the
(6)

table…until we heard a huge crash. My raccoon was

running through the restaurant with _____ in his paws
(7)

and _____ in his fur. Raccoons don't belong in a
(8)

restaurant!

© Learning Resources, Inc.

Grammar Ad Libs 5

Think of a word for each category, and write it on the line.

1. adjective: _____

2. adverb: _____

3. noun (thing): _____

4. verb: _____

5. plural noun (things): _____

6. adverb: _____

7. preposition: _____

8. verb: _____

Photography

Photography is a _____ hobby that you can learn
                    (1)

_____. All you need is a camera, a tripod, and a
 (2)

_____. Once you _____ this equipment, you
 (3)   (4)

should find people, plants, and _____ to
                                    (5)

photograph. Set your tripod _____ _____ a
                              (6)   (7)

flat surface, load your film into your camera, and

_____.
 (8)

Grammar Ad Libs   © Learning Resources, Inc.

Grammar Ad Libs 6 Warm-Up

Choose one word from each group, and circle it.

1. preposition: within in inside

2. adjective: super unique great

3. adverb: cautiously noisily energetically

4. adjective: full wet thick

5. preposition: under below beneath

6. plural noun (things): bugs tigers fish

7. noun (thing): toaster blanket bathtub

Our Jungle Safari

I was very surprised when my parents told me we were

going on a safari deep _____ the jungles of South
                              (1)

America for a _____ vacation. We spent days
                    (2)

_____ driving through _____ jungles, looking
   (3)   (4)

for lizards, parrots, and monkeys. We slept _____
                                                 (5)

the stars, which would have been nice if the _____
                                                  (6)

hadn't bitten us so frequently! The safari was fun, but I

was sure glad to get home to my very own _____
                                              (7)

again.

© Learning Resources, Inc.

Grammar Ad Libs 6

Think of a word for each category, and write it on the line.

1. verb: _____

2. verb: _____

3. preposition: _____

4. silly noise: _____

5. adjective: _____

6. adverb: _____

7. adjective: _____

8. noun (thing): _____

Going to the Doctor

Sometimes you get sick and have to _____ to the

____(1)____

doctor's office. Your doctor may _____ _____

____(2)_____(3)____

your heart, and look at your ears, nose, and throat. She

may even ask you to say "_____." Your doctor will

____(4)____

tell you about your _____ illness and what type of

____(5)____

medicine to take. You should be sure to listen _____

____(6)____

to everything she says, so you aren't _____ when

____(7)____

you get back home to rest in your _____.

____(8)____

 © Learning Resources, Inc.

Name:_____

Grammar Ad Libs 7

Think of a word for each category, and write it on the line.

1. adjective: _____

2. adverb: _____

3. noun (thing): _____

4. adjective: _____

5. plural noun (things): _____

6. preposition: _____

7. adverb: _____

8. adjective: _____

The Mysterious Map

One Saturday, Elana found a _____map stuffed
(1)

_____ behind an old _____ in the attic. She
(2)   (3)

smoothed out the map and saw four _____
(4)

_____ on the map. What did they mean? Could
(5)

they stand for buried treasure? Gold? Jewels? Just then,

Elana's brother Max climbed _____ the attic. "Oh.
(6)

You found my map," he said _____. "I drew that for
(7)

a school project last year." Elana was very _____.
(8)

© Learning Resources, Inc.